Original title:
With Every Step

Copyright © 2024 Swan Charm
All rights reserved.

Author: Kätriin Kaldaru
ISBN HARDBACK: 978-9916-79-084-7
ISBN PAPERBACK: 978-9916-79-085-4
ISBN EBOOK: 978-9916-79-086-1

The Spiral of Experience

Around we twirl in life's vast dance,
Learning truths by chance and circumstance.
With each turn, new layers we find,
Wisdom grows as we unwind.

Moments sparkling in the sun,
Memories weave, becoming one.
In the spiral, joy and strife,
Together they shape our life.

When Paths Converge

Two roads meet under twilight's glow,
Two souls destined, yet unknown.
With hesitant steps, they draw near,
A shared journey begins here.

Stories merge, hearts intertwine,
In this moment, stars align.
Together they craft a new way,
As shadows fade, bright words stay.

Grace in Motion

In every step, grace finds a place,
A gentle touch in life's warm embrace.
Through trials and tempests, we dance,
Balance found in every chance.

With open hearts, we learn to flow,
Letting go of fear and woe.
Like rivers winding through the land,
Grace guides us with a steady hand.

The Expedition of Life

Off we sail on life's grand quest,
With hearts aflame, we seek the best.
Mountains high and valleys low,
Through every challenge, we will grow.

With courage bright, we face the night,
And in the dark, find sparks of light.
Each twist and turn, a tale to tell,
In this adventure, we find our spell.

Steps Beyond the Horizon

Beyond the hills where the sun does rise,
A path unfolds under vibrant skies.
With every step, new dreams take flight,
Chasing shadows into the night.

The world awakens with colors bright,
Soft whispers dance in morning light.
Footprints trace stories left behind,
Echoes of laughter, and love entwined.

Waves of hope crash upon the shore,
Each heartbeat yearns to explore more.
Beneath the sky, wide and free,
We find the truth of what we can be.

Mountains loom, yet we feel no fright,
For every challenge ignites our light.
Together we venture, hand in hand,
Mapping dreams across this land.

In the distance, the horizon glows,
A promise of wonders no one knows.
With each step, we forge our fate,
Unraveling stories, we celebrate.

Winding Trails and Tales

On winding trails through forests deep,
Nature's secrets softly creep.
Whispers of legends, old and wise,
Await our hearts and yearning eyes.

Each twist and turn tells tales anew,
Of moonlit nights and morning dew.
With wildflowers blooming along the way,
The beauty of life invites us to stay.

In shadowed glades where silence sings,
We feel the pulse of all living things.
A gentle breeze, a rustling leaf,
Reminds us to seek beyond belief.

As sunlight pours through branches high,
We chase our dreams up to the sky.
With kindred spirits at our side,
We forge our path, no need to hide.

The trails may twist, the road may bend,
But every journey has its end.
With stories etched in every heart,
We gather memories, never to part.

The Melody of a Trek

Beneath the whispering trees,
Footsteps hum a soft refrain.
Each breeze carries tales untold,
Rhythms of the earth's own song.

Paths winding through the golden fields,
Echoes of the past resound.
Nature's chorus, wild and free,
Calls the heart to wander on.

Mountains rise with silent grace,
Guardians of the skies above.
In their shadows, dreams take flight,
Guided by the stars' bright glow.

Every step a heartbeat felt,
The journey shapes the soul within.
Melodies of courage soar,
As the world unfolds its map.

In the twilight's gentle arms,
The trek finds peace, a sweet embrace.
Each moment sings a quiet tune,
The melody of life goes on.

Grounded Dreams

Roots sink deep in rich black soil,
Where dreams are planted, nurtured slow.
Time dances on a steady beat,
Waves of hope begin to flow.

In the sunlight, thoughts take flight,
Carried by the wind's soft breath.
Every leaf whispers a wish,
Grounded dreams defy their death.

Branches stretch towards the stars,
Craving heights they long to seek.
A tapestry of visions blooms,
Colors bright, yet spirits meek.

Nature's canvas paints the heart,
Brushstrokes of a life well lived.
In the shadows, strength emerges,
Grounded dreams, a gift to give.

Through the seasons, change will come,
Roots and branches, intertwined.
In every challenge, beauty shows,
Grounded dreams will always bind.

The Trail of Tomorrow

Every footfall marks a choice,
In the dust of paths untraveled.
Hope ignites with fervent voice,
On the trail where dreams unravel.

Stars above guide the wayfarer,
Whispers shared with the rising sun.
Each dawn brings new horizons near,
The trail of tomorrow's begun.

Winding roads and hidden turns,
Secrets wrapped in nature's hands.
In the heart, a feeling burns,
Future laid like shifting sands.

Step by step, with faith as clutch,
Carving out a world anew.
Every moment, tender touch,
On the trail, where dreams come true.

In the quiet of the night,
Courage swells like tide's embrace.
On the path, we seek the light,
The trail of tomorrow's grace.

Wandering Between Worlds

In the space where shadows play,
Fractured light sings soft and low.
Between the realms where dreamers stray,
Reality begins to flow.

Whispers of an ancient song,
Floating through the twilight mist.
Here, the lost and found belong,
In the folds of what exists.

Branches twist to bridge the gap,
Connecting all that cannot be.
Every thought a woven map,
Lost in time, yet wild and free.

Colors clash in vibrant hues,
Painting dreams that shimmer bright.
Each world holds its own views,
Wandering between day and night.

In the stillness, echoes play,
Hearts entwined in mystic dance.
Exploring realms, they drift away,
Wandering, they find their chance.

Unveiling New Paths

The dawn breaks softly, light unfolds,
A journey beckons, whispers untold.
With every step, a tale unwinds,
In the heart of the seeker, freedom binds.

Mountains loom high, valleys lie low,
Through tangled woods, adventurers go.
Each choice a brushstroke, vivid and bright,
On the canvas of life, a beautiful sight.

Rivers of dreams flow, deep and wide,
With courage as compass, and hope as guide.
The path may twist, the road may bend,
But onward we march, towards the end.

Faces and places, all intertwine,
In the dance of fate, a story divine.
With every heartbeat, with every breath,
We unveil new paths, defying death.

The Whisper of Wheels

A soft hum rises, the engine purrs,
Through endless roads, the traveler stirs.
The world rushes by, a vivid blur,
In the comfort of seats, emotions stir.

Windows rolled down, the breeze in hair,
Every mile traveled, memories share.
As wheels spin round, life's rhythm plays,
In the song of the journey, we find our ways.

Fields of gold pass, and mountains loom tall,
Concrete jungles, where echoes call.
The whisper of wheels, a tranquil sound,
In the dance of the road, lost souls are found.

With laughter and tears, the essence flows,
In the heart of the traveler, adventure grows.
Every stop a story, every turn a chance,
In the rhythm of travel, we find our dance.

Dancing Alongside Destiny

In the twilight glow, we find our feet,
The music of life holds a vibrant beat.
With every twirl, the stars align,
In the hands of fate, our dreams entwine.

Moments like raindrops, glistening bright,
They gather together, a marvelous sight.
With laughter and grace, we step in time,
Dancing through shadows, our spirits climb.

Through paths unknown, we make our way,
With courage in our hearts, unafraid to sway.
For destiny waits, with open arms,
In the dance of the cosmos, we find our charms.

With each heartbeat, we follow the call,
The rhythm of life, a mesmerizing thrall.
So take my hand, and together we'll sing,
Dancing alongside the joy that fate brings.

Shadows Underfoot

In the quiet dusk, when day turns night,
Shadows arise, stealing the light.
They dance upon paths, both dark and bright,
In the arms of the twilight, mysteries ignite.

Footsteps echo softly, whispers of time,
In the stories we tread, we form the rhyme.
With every shadow, a memory stays,
In the corners of life, where silence plays.

Branches weave shadows, tales they unfold,
Of dreams lost and found, of love uncontrolled.
Beneath the stillness, we pulse and breathe,
In the shadows underfoot, we learn to believe.

So walk with me here, where shadows entwine,
In the twilight's embrace, our hopes align.
For every shadow, a beauty does hide,
In the dance of existence, we share this ride.

The Journey Within

In silence, whispers beckon me,
To realms where thoughts roam free.
A map unwritten, a path unseen,
Exploring depths that softly gleam.

Each step unfolds a hidden truth,
Where shadows dance, unearths my youth.
The heart's compass steers me right,
Through tangled woods, into the light.

The echoes of my past collide,
With dreams that swell like ocean tide.
In every heartbeat, a new refrain,
My spirit soars, unbroken chain.

I tread the trails of hope and dread,
With courage forged from words unsaid.
In every mirror, I find my soul,
A puzzle piece that makes me whole.

This journey deep will never cease,
In every moment, I find peace.
The unfolding pages of my core,
Lead me to discover evermore.

Footsteps in the Breeze

Lightly dancing, thoughts take flight,
Footsteps whisper in the night.
The gentle breeze hums a tune,
As memories twirl beneath the moon.

Each step a story, softly spun,
In twilight's glow, the day is done.
The world awakens, colors blend,
Where paths converge, my heart will mend.

Amidst the rustle of the leaves,
I find the strength that nature weaves.
With every stride, my soul aligns,
In this soft realm where laughter shines.

So I shall wander, chase the light,
With open arms and heart so bright.
Through every season, every breeze,
I'll trace the footsteps, feel the ease.

For in each moment, life does speak,
In whispers soft, in silence meek.
A journey woven with the sky,
In footsteps light, I learn to fly.

The Pulse of Progress

In cities bustling, dreams ignite,
The pulse of progress, day and night.
With every heartbeat, change unfolds,
A tapestry of stories told.

From cobblestones to towers high,
Innovation soars, and spirits fly.
With passion fierce, the vision grows,
In every challenge, potential glows.

The rhythm of the future calls,
In every rise, in every fall.
With hands joined tight, we pave the way,
To brighter dreams, a new today.

Through trials faced, we learn to stand,
With hope that we can understand.
In unity, our voices blend,
A symphony that will not end.

The pulse of life, a beating drum,
Through tides of change, we will become.
Together writing history bold,
In every heart, a story told.

Imprints on Infinity

Beneath the stars, where dreams are spun,
Imprints linger, lessons won.
In whispers soft, the cosmos sighs,
A dance of time that never dies.

In fleeting moments, memories trace,
The echoes of a boundless space.
Each heartbeat writes a tale anew,
In twilight's glow, in morning's dew.

The universe holds every breath,
In shadowed corners, life and death.
Through galaxies, our spirits soar,
With every pulse, we crave for more.

In every tear, in every laugh,
The imprints weave our cosmic path.
A tapestry interlinked so tight,
With threads of love that shine so bright.

As we explore this vast expanse,
The dance of fate, a timeless trance.
In infinite space, we find our place,
Forever imprinted in time and grace.

Beneath the Burden of Soles

Heavy steps on weary ground,
Each echo a story profound.
Soles worn thin, yet spirits rise,
Beneath the sun, beneath the skies.

Dusty trails and whispered fears,
The burden borne through days and years.
With every stride, new strength is found,
In the journey's heart, I'm unbound.

Footprints mark the paths we've tread,
Tales of laughter, love, and dread.
As shadows stretch and daylight fades,
We carry on through life's charades.

Nature sings the songs of old,
In every crack, a story told.
With gratitude, I take my stance,
Beneath the weight of fate's own dance.

Together we walk, hand in hand,
Face the storms, we understand.
The burden shared makes lighter loads,
In unity, our spirit glows.

In the Footsteps of Giants

Many walked where I now roam,
In giants' shadows, I find home.
Their echoes linger in the air,
A legacy, silent and rare.

Ancient trees with stories wrapped,
In whispered winds, their wisdom tapped.
Through valleys deep, and mountains high,
I forge ahead, beneath the sky.

Every rock, a memory keeps,
In nature's heart, the knowledge seeps.
Honoring those who came before,
Each step I take, I seek for more.

Their dreams a compass, guiding me,
In every heartbeat, I am free.
Finding strength in those who stood,
In the shadows, I feel their good.

With humility, I press on,
In their footsteps, I am drawn.
A tapestry of past interlace,
In the giants' trails, I find my place.

Journeying Through Time

Footprints in the sands of time,
Each a moment, each a rhyme.
Seasons change, the clock unwinds,
Stories echo, knowledge binds.

In the corridors of the past,
Wisdom glimmers, futures cast.
Through the ages, we explore,
Windows open, seeking more.

Time a river, flowing free,
Carrying dreams, both you and me.
In threads of history, we find,
A mosaic of the human kind.

Moments captured, memories shared,
In a tapestry, we are ensnared.
As pages turn in life's own book,
With every glance, new paths we took.

Journeying forth, a dance of fate,
Embracing love, we celebrate.
In the realm beyond the now,
Time whispers softly, take a bow.

Shifting Sands of Experience

On shifting sands, we make our way,
Each grain a truth in disarray.
Lessons learned in every plight,
With every stumble, we find light.

The winds of change shape all we know,
In tempest's howl, new seeds we sow.
With courage found in fragile trust,
We rise again, as rise we must.

Reflections cast in dunes of gold,
Stories of the brave and bold.
Through trials faced and dreams pursued,
In the journey's heart, we are renewed.

Through tides of time, we navigate,
Embracing love, defying fate.
In each wave, a lesson flows,
Shifting sands, where wisdom grows.

With open hearts, we greet the dawn,
In shifting sands, our spirits drawn.
Together we rise, in unity's grace,
Finding our strength in every place.

Each Footfall Counts

In every step we take, a story unfolds,
Worn paths beneath us, their secrets retold.
With each footfall, memories linger,
Whispers of journeys, soft as a singer.

The ground hums gently, a rhythm divine,
Each stride a heartbeat, perfectly timed.
Moments connect in the dance of the now,
Bearing our burdens, yet teaching us how.

In the forest or city, each step is a choice,
Echoes of purpose, in silence, they voice.
Through gravel and grass, through mud and through stone,
Every footfall a blessing, reminding we're not alone.

With every new venture, the past we reflect,
Footfalls that guide us, we learn to respect.
So tread with intention, each path that we find,
For every footfall counts, with purpose aligned.

Balancing on the Edge

Life's a tightrope, wobbly and fine,
Where dreams dance lightly on a fragile line.
Each moment a choice, to sway or to fall,
Balancing boldly, we heed the call.

We walk through the shadows, our fears held tight,
The edge calls our name in the pale morning light.
With courage our anchor, we step forth with grace,
Searching for meaning in this daring space.

Risking the plunge, though the ground seems far,
We find in the journey, just who we are.
The thrill of the challenge, the breath of the fight,
Dancing on boundaries, we bask in the height.

In laughter and tears, we find our own way,
Each moment a treasure, no reason to sway.
So balance on edges, let your spirit fly,
In the dance of the daring, we learn how to try.

Paths Poetry Paints

In lines of soft verses, the landscapes unfold,
Paths marked by the heartbeat, in stories retold.
With ink like a river, emotions collide,
Each stanza a journey, where visions abide.

The hills breathe a sonnet, the valleys a rhyme,
Tracing the footsteps, through space and through time.
A canvas of feelings, brushed lightly with care,
Every word is a stepping stone, leading us there.

Through forests of metaphor, we wander at will,
Where whispers of wisdom rise up from the quill.
The trails that we travel, uncharted yet clear,
Each path that we follow, we hold ever dear.

In starlit reflections, we gather our dreams,
The world is a poem, or so it seems.
Let each line be a pathway through dusk and through dawn,
For the paths that we paint, lead us ever on.

The Soundtrack of Movement

With every footstep, a rhythm is made,
The world's symphony plays, in light and in shade.
A shuffle of leaves, the hush of the air,
The soundtrack of movement, a dance we all share.

The city's heartbeat, a pulsing refrain,
Echoes of laughter, and whispers of rain.
In the stride of our lives, the tempo unfolds,
With stories unwritten, as each moment unfolds.

We sway with the music of heartbeats in sync,
In the flow of the moment, we find time to think.
The bounce of ambition, the glide of release,
In the soundtrack of movement, we discover our peace.

So let every motion, be graced with a tune,
A melody woven by sun and by moon.
For through every rhythm, our spirits will soar,
In the soundtrack of movement, forever explore.

Unraveling the Way

In shadows deep, we seek the light,
Each twist reveals a path so bright.
With every turn, new tales arise,
Truth unfolds beneath the skies.

Lost in moments, yet we find,
A map within, a filigree mind.
Connections made, the threads align,
In this journey, we intertwine.

The whispers of past echo near,
Carrying hope, dissolving fear.
We tread the soil of dreams once sown,
In nature's cradle, we feel at home.

As seasons change, we gently sway,
Embracing all that comes our way.
With every heartbeat, we explore,
The boundless love that we adore.

Through winding roads and open doors,
We dance in rhythm, find our cores.
Each step a testament to grace,
In this vast life, we find our place.

Steps Through the Seasons

Winter's hush blankets the ground,
In silence raw, new dreams are found.
Snowflakes swirl in whispered cheer,
A promise kept, that spring draws near.

Spring awakens with vibrant hues,
Blossoms bloom, the world imbues.
In gentle rains, our hopes take flight,
Chasing shadows, igniting light.

Summer sun, a blazing ray,
Where laughter echoes through the day.
Fields alive with colors bright,
Each heartbeat syncs with pure delight.

Autumn arrives with golden glow,
Leaves surrender, a graceful flow.
In each crinkle, stories told,
Memories captured, neverold.

Through seasons' dance, we find the grace,
In every change, we embrace our place.
Life's circle spins, a wondrous show,
In every step, the heart will grow.

A Continuous Voyage

A ship sets sail on endless tides,
With dreams that pull like evening rides.
The stars above, our compass true,
Guide us to shores we never knew.

Waves may crash, and storms may roar,
Yet hope remains, a steadfast core.
With every wave, a story spins,
Through azure vastness, our journey begins.

Islands rise, like whispers found,
In silence deep, our hearts unbound.
Through trade winds swift, we chart our way,
In unity's strength, we choose to stay.

Clouds may gather, but skies will clear,
We'll sail through doubts, conquer fear.
With sails unfurled, we'll dance in light,
In every heart, a spark ignites.

As horizons blend, our spirits soar,
With every drift, we crave for more.
A journey endless, a tale untold,
In every heartbeat, our dreams unfold.

Heartbeats on the Trail

Footsteps echo on a winding track,
Each heartbeat sings, with no turning back.
Together we tread on nature's floor,
In every breath, our spirits soar.

Mountains rise, like guardians deep,
Promises made, in silence keep.
With every climb, a challenge met,
The bond we forge, we won't forget.

Streams that dance through sunlit glade,
Nature's rhythm, our worries fade.
With every ripple, a laugh takes flight,
In harmony with day and night.

Whispers of leaves in breeze we hear,
Carried on, we have no fear.
With every step, we write our song,
In the embrace of nature, we belong.

Stars will guide us on our way,
In every heart, a light will stay.
Together we will carve our day,
Through every trail, we find our way.

Walking Through Wonders

In the hush of early dawn,
Colors dance, a vivid song.
Nature whispers, secrets shared,
As the world awakens, unprepared.

Petals glow in morning light,
Every leaf, a heart in flight.
Soft winds carry tales untold,
In this magic, feel the bold.

Streams that sparkle, rivers gleam,
Every moment feels like a dream.
Mountains stand, a watchful eye,
Underneath the endless sky.

Footsteps echo on sunlit trails,
Stories linger where love prevails.
With every step, I breathe the air,
In these wonders, hearts laid bare.

Time flows like the flowing sea,
In this place, I feel so free.
Wonders greet me at every turn,
A world alive, forever to learn.

Ground Beneath My Soles

The ground beneath, a canvas wide,
Each step a mark, a gentle guide.
Soft and firm, it holds my weight,
A testament to moments great.

Pebbles whisper of journeys past,
Reminding me that nothing's vast.
Roots entangle, deep and strong,
In this place, I belong.

Grass tickles toes, warm sun above,
The earth cradles all I love.
Each footfall sings, a silent song,
In this space where I feel strong.

Clouds drift lazily, shadows play,
On this ground, I wish to stay.
Beneath my soles, a world unfolds,
Every tale, a treasure told.

Ground beneath, my steady base,
In each path, I find my place.
In every crack and every fold,
Stories linger, vibrant and bold.

Each Footprint a Memory

Footprints etched upon the shore,
Whispers of the days before.
Every stride, a tale to tell,
In the silence, memories swell.

Sand beneath my wandering feet,
Reminds me of adventures sweet.
With each mark, I leave a trace,
In this moment, I find grace.

Paths of laughter, roads of tears,
Capture echoes of my years.
Each footprint tells of joys and fears,
Crafting stories through the years.

Sunrise glow or twilight's hue,
Each step recalls a dream anew.
In every line, a part of me,
Carved in earth, forever free.

I walk on, as shadows blend,
With every step, the journey bends.
Each footprint a memory to hold,
In the heart, a world of gold.

Steps into Tomorrow

With every step, I venture forth,
Into the dawn, a promise worth.
The path ahead, unknown and bright,
Guided by the morning light.

Horizon stretches, dreams take flight,
Each stride ignites the hopeful night.
With courage, fears begin to fade,
In the present, futures laid.

Steps align with heartbeats strong,
Every moment, where I belong.
Beyond the doubts, the shadows chase,
I find my place, my own embrace.

In between the breaths we make,
New beginnings, chances take.
Tomorrow waits with open arms,
In its beauty, endless charms.

With vision clear and spirits high,
I step into the vast blue sky.
Each footfall leads to paths unknown,
In this journey, I am home.

Steps into Silence

In the calm of twilight's glow,
Footfalls whisper soft and slow.
Each step marked on the earth,
Echoes telling tales of worth.

Shadows drift and shadows blend,
In this place where dreams descend.
Breath is gentle, hearts awake,
In the silence, we partake.

Stillness wraps the world in peace,
Finding comfort, sweet release.
Time stands still, a fleeting grace,
In the quiet's warm embrace.

Voices muted, thoughts align,
As moon and stars begin to shine.
Each heartbeat is a love song,
In this silence, we belong.

Steps dissolve into the night,
Guided by the soft starlight.
In this dance, we fade away,
Leaving traces where we play.

The Quiet Dance of Movement

In the stillness, shadows sway,
Whispers weave the night away.
Hands released, the world turns slow,
In this dance, we learn to flow.

Bodies twirl in soft embrace,
Graceful lines through empty space.
Every motion tells a story,
In quiet steps, we find our glory.

Time drifts by like falling leaves,
Hidden truths the silence weaves.
In this moment, lost and found,
Harmony within the sound.

Eyes closed tight, we feel the beat,
Connecting hearts in soft retreat.
Glimmers of a life well spun,
In the quiet, we are one.

As we move, the world stands still,
Dancing softly, hearts refill.
In this motion, life unfolds,
The quiet dance of hearts so bold.

A Journey of Heartbeats

Each heartbeat is a step we take,
Through valleys deep and skies that shake.
With every pulse, a tale we tell,
Of love and loss where memories dwell.

The rhythm guides, both wild and free,
An echo of our destiny.
With every breath, we forge ahead,
Along the paths, our spirits led.

In moments fleeting, close your eyes,
Feel the whispers, hear the sighs.
Time unwinds like threads of gold,
Stories precious, yet untold.

Together we march, hand in hand,
Through shifting skies and shifting sand.
Every heartbeat sings a song,
In the journey where we belong.

With each thump, a promise made,
In the silence, unafraid.
A life of wonders, bright and stark,
A journey lit by every spark.

Traced in Time

Footprints fade as tides reclaim,
The sands of time, they know our name.
In the distance, echoes call,
Signatures on history's wall.

Moments linger on the breeze,
Catching whispers through the trees.
In the autumn's gentle sigh,
Life's circle spins and we comply.

With every season, shadows grow,
Memories in moonlit glow.
Each star a tale, a wish, a dream,
In this vast and endless theme.

Time our canvas, strokes of fate,
Weaving paths, both small and great.
Each heartbeat markers on the line,
In this journey, traced in time.

As we wander, paths will blur,
Yet in our hearts, we always stir.
Connected through the threads we find,
Ever woven, hearts aligned.

The Road Beckons Gently

The winding path calls out to me,
Beneath the whispering trees.
Sunlight dances through the leaves,
Where the heart quietly believes.

Steps taken with gentle grace,
Along the trail of dreams we chase.
With every turn, a story spun,
In the glow of the setting sun.

Fleeting moments softly shared,
In this place, we are prepared.
To wander where the wildflowers grow,
And let our spirits freely flow.

Each footfall on this sacred ground,
In nature's lap, our souls are found.
A journey with no need to hurry,
As the road beckons with sweet flurry.

So here we stand, no fear to roam,
For in this world, we find our home.
Together, we shall find our way,
As the road beckons, come what may.

A Stroll Through Shadows

Beneath the boughs where shadows play,
A serene path leads us away.
Whispers of night brush past our skin,
Where the daylight begins to thin.

Every step feels like a dance,
As the moonlight gives its glance.
Echoes of footsteps linger near,
In the quiet, we'll have no fear.

We find our way through thickets wild,
Nature's embrace, tender and mild.
The cool breeze carries secrets old,
In the twilight's gentle hold.

With each shadow, a story grows,
In the dark, the true magic glows.
Weaving dreams and memories bright,
In the hush of the coming night.

So let us stroll through shadows deep,
Where the world around us sleeps.
In the silence, our hearts will blend,
On this journey that has no end.

The Echoing Journey

In the distance, echoes call,
Guiding us through the rise and fall.
Each step we take, a note in time,
A blend of rhythm and rhyme.

Mountains stand with stories to tell,
In the vastness, we find ourselves.
With every path, a chance to see,
The echoes of who we can be.

Voices carried on the breeze,
In their tones, there's solace and ease.
We'll wander far, explore the sound,
In these echoes, we are unbound.

Through valleys deep and skies so wide,
Nature is our faithful guide.
With each experience, we grow,
As the echoes bend and flow.

So let us chase what lies ahead,
With courage found, no need for dread.
In the echoing journey, we create,
A tapestry of love and fate.

Pathways of Possibility

Along the paths where futures rise,
Beneath the ever-changing skies.
Each road a choice, a tale untold,
In the dreams we dare to hold.

Twisting routes unbound by fear,
With every step, the vision clear.
Paths of hope and light await,
Led by dreams we dare to create.

With hearts ablaze, we forge ahead,
Onwards to where our dreams are fed.
In every journey lies a chance,
To find our voice, to sing, to dance.

With open minds and endless hearts,
We'll make our mark through countless starts.
For life is but a winding stream,
Flowing on pathways of possibility and dream.

So let us walk with purpose bright,
In the dawn of day, in the depth of night.
For each direction brings us near,
To the futures we hold dear.

As We Move On

With each step, we leave behind,
The echoes of a time well-spent.
We'll carry forth what we have learned,
In hearts where memories are meant.

The road ahead is wide and bright,
With shadows fading, dreams take flight.
We forge ahead, hand in hand,
Together we will make our stand.

The whispers of our past will guide,
As we embrace the great unknown.
Each twist and turn, a chance to grow,
In every seed of hope we've sown.

Our voices blend, a melody,
Through valleys deep, and hills so high.
United in this journey's path,
We'll face each moment, let dreams fly.

So here we stand, with open hearts,
As we begin a brand new page.
The future calls, so let us run,
Embracing every dawn, no cage.

Treading New Grounds

On fields of green, we take our stand,
With every step, we dare to dream.
Together, hearts and minds expand,
Creating futures, brighter beams.

Through spaces where the wild winds blow,
We find our strength in unity.
Each path we tread begins to show,
The limitless we've yet to see.

In shaded woods, we pause and rest,
The sun breaks through, a guiding light.
With open arms, we feel the best,
As courage fuels our hopeful flight.

With every heartbeat, risks we take,
We carve our names on ancient stones.
In every choice, the new we make,
We weave a tale that's all our own.

The ground we tread is rich and wide,
For dreams that shape the world we seek.
Treading new grounds, side by side,
With every moment, bold and unique.

In the Wake of Dreams

In quiet night, where shadows play,
The dreams we chase begin to brew.
With every heartbeat, night turns day,
In fragile hopes, we feel anew.

Through starlit paths, our spirits soar,
With whispers lacing through the air.
In the wake of dreams, we explore,
With open minds, we dare and care.

The visions dance, elusive light,
Along the shores of what could be.
We're drawn to quests, our hearts ignite,
In unity, we'll sail the sea.

Each goal a pebble, skip and throw,
We'll watch them ripple, reach the shore.
In the wake of dreams, we'll grow,
And cherish all we long for more.

So here we stand, with eyes aglow,
In the wake of dreams we chase.
Together bound, we'll rise and flow,
Creating time and sacred space.

Steps Across Time

With every step, we weave a tale,
Of moments lost and ones to find.
Each footfall strikes a vibrant trail,
As past and present intertwine.

The echoes of our laughter ring,
Across the years, we hum a tune.
In every heart, a rhythm springs,
To guide us closer to the moon.

Through winding paths, we search for truth,
The lessons etched on timeless clay.
In dreams of youth and shades of youth,
We paint the skies in hues of gray.

In steps across, the ages meet,
With stories written in our veins.
Time bends for dreams, in gentle feat,
Uniting hearts through joy and pains.

So here we stand, with hands entwined,
Steps across time, forever free.
In every glance, the stars aligned,
We write our fate, just you and me.

The Pursuit of Tomorrow

Chasing dreams in morning light,
Hopes arise, taking flight.
In the distance, futures gleam,
A tapestry of every dream.

With every step, we find our way,
Building bridges toward the day.
Whispers of hope guide the heart,
In this journey, we take part.

Through shadows cast by doubt and fear,
Voices whisper, 'Persevere.'
The road ahead may twist and turn,
Yet with each lesson, we discern.

The sun may set, but stars will shine,
In night's embrace, our hearts entwine.
Navigating paths both near and wide,
In pursuit of tomorrow, we abide.

Together we rise, hand in hand,
United in dreams, we take a stand.
The future beckons, bright and clear,
On the horizon, our purpose near.

A Cascade of Moments

Moments tumble like a stream,
Each one precious, bright with dreams.
Time dances lightly down the lane,
Every heartbeat, joy or pain.

Laughter echoes, memories flow,
In the current, we learn to grow.
Captured glances, soft embraces,
Every memory, time retraces.

From dawn's light to dusk's end,
Each instant, a message we send.
Like leaves that spin in autumn's breeze,
Cherished moments, aim to please.

In a gallery of our days,
Our hearts weave stories in myriad ways.
A symphony of now and then,
A cascade of moments, again and again.

So let us savor what we find,
In fleeting seconds, love's refined.
For in this dance of time's embrace,
Moments linger, a warm trace.

The Dance of Distance

Miles stretch like a silent song,
Yet in our hearts, we still belong.
Across the void, your voice I hear,
In every whisper, you are near.

Time zones shift, the world expands,
Yet our love bridges distant lands.
With every star that lights the night,
A reminder of our shared delight.

In absence, memories intertwine,
Creating bonds that brightly shine.
Each text, a step, each call, a chance,
In this vast space, we find our dance.

The sky may darken, storms may rise,
But hope shines bright in shared skies.
Embracing distance, we stay true,
In every heartbeat, I find you.

Together we conquer ocean's might,
In dreams, we travel, souls take flight.
For love, my dear, can bridge all space,
In the dance of distance, we find grace.

Onward Through the Unknown

The path ahead, a mystery vast,
With every step, shadows are cast.
Yet courage blooms where fears reside,
Onward we tread, hearts open wide.

With stars to guide in darkest hours,
We seek our truth among the flowers.
Each winding road, a story told,
In each pause, a dream unfolds.

The whispers of fate call out our name,
As we venture forth to play the game.
In pauses linger, doubts may sway,
Yet hope ignites the path each day.

Through trials faced and mountains climbed,
In unity, we find the rhyme.
For every stumble, a chance to rise,
Onward we go, towards the skies.

So hand in hand, we forge ahead,
With dreams as sails, our fears we shed.
In the embrace of the great unknown,
Together we journey, never alone.

The Tapestry of Travels

In distant lands where stories meet,
Each step we take feels bittersweet.
A tapestry of heart and grace,
We weave our dreams in every place.

With every sunrise, wonders bloom,
In markets bright, in evening's gloom.
The whispers of the wind to hear,
Guide us onward, year by year.

Through mountains high and valleys low,
We gather treasures, much to show.
Each face we meet a tale to share,
In this grand world, a love affair.

Beneath the stars, we find our song,
A melody where we belong.
Our journeys blend in colors bold,
A story rich, a treasure told.

And when at last we find our way,
A patchwork quilt of night and day.
With hearts entwined, we've come so far,
A journey traced beneath each star.

Navigating New Beginnings

With dawn anew, we take our flight,
On paths unknown, towards the light.
Each heartbeat calls, a whisper clear,
Embrace the change, let go of fear.

The dawn invites us to explore,
Beyond the shores, beyond the door.
In every challenge, hope will bloom,
A brilliant flower in the gloom.

Moments lost are moments gained,
With every high, embrace the pain.
Step boldly forth, let courage swell,
For every story, there's a spell.

Let dreams take shape like clouds above,
In swirling winds, we find our love.
The future beckons, bright and grand,
In unity, we take a stand.

Though change may shake the ground we tread,
New seeds of trust are gently spread.
With every breath, we rise, ascend,
In unity, we find a friend.

Steps Over Stones

On sturdy feet, we forge our way,
Through crags and rocks, come what may.
Each stone we pass, a tale we tell,
Of trials faced, of how we fell.

The path is rough, with bends and turns,
A dance of fate, where passion burns.
We lift our gaze to skies above,
With every step, we learn to love.

In shadows deep, the light does gleam,
A flicker bright, a distant dream.
As rivers flow and seasons change,
Our journey blooms, it feels so strange.

We stumble, yet we rise once more,
Through every sigh, we learn to soar.
With hearts ablaze, we chase the dawn,
In unity, we march along.

For every stone that blocks our path,
We gather strength, we face the wrath.
With dreams in sight and hope so strong,
Together, we will right the wrong.

The Language of Movement

In silence found, our bodies speak,
With every turn, with every peak.
A rhythm born from pulse and breath,
We dance through life, in love and death.

The sway of hips, the reach of hands,
In every step, the heart demands.
A symphony within the soul,
In motion's grace, we become whole.

From gentle paths to daring leaps,
Our story flows, it runs, it sweeps.
With every twirl, we write our fate,
A journey shared, a dance innate.

In whispered vows and laughter bright,
We find our way through day and night.
The dance of life, a sacred art,
In fluid grace, we join the heart.

So let us move, let spirits soar,
In timeless dance, forevermore.
The language speaks, in every glance,
Together bound in this sweet dance.

The Tread of Hope

In the dawn's golden hue,
Dreams take their flight,
With each step we choose,
Hope shines so bright.

Through valleys of doubt,
We rise and we climb,
With courage as fuel,
Our spirits in rhyme.

The road may be long,
Yet we're never alone,
With hearts that can sing,
Together we've grown.

In whispers of courage,
With every small stride,
We find our own strength,
With hope as our guide.

So let the world turn,
Beneath our bold feet,
For in every heartbeat,
Life's rhythm, we meet.

In Search of New Horizons

Across the endless sea,
We sail with our dreams,
In search of the stars,
And new morning beams.

With winds in our sails,
Our spirits ascend,
Each wave tells a tale,
Of journeys that bend.

Through storms we will brave,
Each challenge we face,
For treasures await,
In the vast open space.

The horizon calls softly,
With whispers so sweet,
Promising wonder,
And adventure to greet.

So onward we venture,
With hearts full of fire,
For life is a canvas,
And hope is our choir.

Footprints of Fireflies

In fields where they dance,
The fireflies glow,
Leaving trails of light,
As night starts to flow.

With whispers of magic,
They twirl in delight,
Painting the darkness,
With flickers of light.

Each tiny spark tells,
Of stories untold,
Of journeys of dreams,
In the night that unfolds.

With a heart full of wonder,
We follow their flight,
Finding our own way,
In the embrace of the night.

So cherish the moments,
When the world shines so bright,
For in the small wonders,
Lies joy and pure light.

Gait of the Brave

With each step we take,
A story unfolds,
In the dance of our lives,
We are fearless and bold.

Through valleys of challenge,
And mountains of dreams,
We carve our own path,
With hopes and with gleams.

For the journey is sacred,
Each heartbeat, a song,
In the dance of the brave,
We truly belong.

With courage as armor,
And faith in our core,
We meet every trial,
And rise to explore.

So take up your banner,
And stride with the light,
For the gait of the brave,
Always shines ever bright.

Sculpture of Soles

In the clay of my dreams,
Footprints trace the past,
Each one tells a story,
Of shadows that are cast.

Weathered by the seasons,
They whisper of the years,
Of paths that led us forward,
Of laughter mixed with tears.

Sculptures made of moments,
In silent monologue,
Each curve a whispered secret,
Each line a gentle fog.

With every step I take,
The earth begins to mold,
An art of my journey,
In memories untold.

So here I stand in wonder,
Among the lines of grace,
A sculpture carved in footsteps,
A timeless, sacred space.

In Search of the Horizon

Chasing dreams of daylight,
I wander far and wide,
With every step I'm searching,
For the sun's golden stride.

The horizon calls my name,
A beacon glowing bright,
It dances on the water,
It lives beyond my sight.

Waves crash against my journey,
Their whispers fill the air,
With tales of distant lands,
And secrets we must share.

In search of a new sunrise,
I walk the sandy shore,
Each moment feels enchanting,
Yet deep I crave for more.

The horizon shifts and falters,
Forever out of reach,
Yet in this quest for meaning,
Life's lessons softly teach.

The Journey Revealed

Paths unfold like stories,
In the quiet of the night,
Each step a new beginning,
Each shadow comes to light.

Mountains high above me,
Rivers winding low,
In this vast expanse,
I find the will to grow.

Every twist and turn I take,
Unwraps a layer true,
The journey reveals more,
Than the destination due.

With lessons etched in silence,
And hopes that intertwine,
The road becomes my mirror,
Reflecting what is mine.

So onward I shall wander,
With heart and soul aligned,
In every breath a promise,
The journey, kind and blind.

Footfalls of Fate

In the dance of chance and choice,
I leave my trace as I roam,
With each footfall on hard ground,
I carve a path called home.

Fate echoes in the silence,
It guides my every move,
Through trials and through triumphs,
Its rhythm helps me groove.

Steps taken in the twilight,
Mark moments where I stand,
Each imprint holds a secret,
A story unplanned.

With courage wrapped in stillness,
And hope within the stride,
I'll follow where it leads me,
With fate my trusted guide.

So I dance with every heartbeat,
Each footfall, bold and brave,
For in the dance of fate I find,
The life that I must save.

Mapping the Heart's Passage

In silence, whispers start to bloom,
Sketching feelings, dispelling gloom.
With every tear, a story flows,
In ink of hope, the journey grows.

Navigating through the inner seas,
Charting dreams on gentle breeze.
A compass made of love and light,
Guiding souls through darkest night.

Each heartbeat echoes in the vast,
Reminders of a love that lasts.
Turning pages of a life well-spent,
In the map, our hearts' consent.

Through valleys deep and mountains high,
We find our way, and never shy.
Beyond the pain, a vibrant start,
In every mark, we trace the heart.

So let us walk on paths defined,
With open hearts, and hopes aligned.
For every step, a chance to feel,
In this journey, love is real.

The Melody of Motion

In every step, a song unfolds,
A dance of dreams, a tale retold.
With each heartbeat, rhythms play,
Echoing love in soft ballet.

Through winding roads, our spirits soar,
Together swaying, forevermore.
The world a stage, and we the stars,
Under the glow of moonlit bars.

Each sway and turn a new refrain,
A symphony of joy and pain.
In life's embrace, we find our song,
In harmony, where hearts belong.

Through whispered notes and laughter bright,
We dance in shadows, we dance in light.
Every step a cherished beat,
In life's grand waltz, we're complete.

So let the music guide our way,
In every moment, come what may.
Together in this sweet devotion,
We write the melody of motion.

Horizons Await

Beyond the waves, the sun does rise,
Painting dreams across the skies.
With every dawn, a chance to start,
As open hearts begin to chart.

Mountains stand tall, whispers of time,
Each peak a promise, every climb.
In valleys deep, new seeds we sow,
With courage found, our spirits grow.

Beneath the stars, our wishes fly,
Carried forth by winds on high.
For in the night, our hopes ignite,
Illuminating paths so bright.

With every step, the horizon calls,
Breaking barriers, tearing walls.
In unity, we'll find our fate,
As love awaits, don't hesitate.

So let us venture, hand in hand,
Through fields of dreams, across the land.
For in our hearts, a truth so great,
Horizons await, let's navigate.

Pathways of Connection

In every glance, a bond is born,
A thread of trust, no longer torn.
With open hearts, we find our way,
On pathways brightly lit by day.

Through laughter shared and tears embraced,
Memories woven, time interlaced.
In every word, a tale we weave,
In moments shared, we dare believe.

Together facing storms that rage,
Finding strength on life's grand stage.
In unity, we rise as one,
In shadows cast, we find the sun.

With every heartbeat, love defined,
In whispered hopes and dreams aligned.
For in connection, we find our grace,
In every soul, a sacred space.

So let us cherish all we share,
In every moment, show we care.
For life's a journey, rich and true,
On pathways of connection, me and you.

Walking the Edge of Dreams

I wander through the twilight haze,
Where whispers of the night-time play.
Fleeting visions brush my mind,
A dance of hopes I've yet to find.

In shadows cast by silver light,
I chase the dreams that stir my flight.
With every step, the heartbeat sings,
A melody of endless things.

The stars above, they guide my way,
As dawn unveils the break of day.
Each heartbeat leads me ever near,
To all the dreams that beckon clear.

I tread the line 'twixt real and true,
Where every wish seems fresh and new.
With open arms, I brave the night,
For visions hold an endless flight.

At last, I find my fragile ground,
In dreams where hope and truth abound.
The edge becomes a place of grace,
Where light and shadow interlace.

Unfolding Horizons

Beyond the hills, the sun does rise,
Its golden rays paint azure skies.
Each dawn reveals a brand new view,
With every step, the world feels new.

The whispers of the wind call me,
To wander wide, to roam so free.
As paths unfold beneath my feet,
Adventure waits on every street.

With heart in hand, I seek the vast,
Eager to learn from ages past.
Horizons stretch beyond the known,
In every shadow, seeds are sown.

I gather tales from distant lands,
And weave them gently with my hands.
In every corner, stories bloom,
Unfolding joy within the room.

The journey calls, a siren's song,
Guiding me where I belong.
With every view, a chance to learn,
Unfolding horizons, hearts that yearn.

Steps into the Unknown

With every step, a choice is made,
Into the dark, past light's cascade.
The path ahead may twist and turn,
A place where courage starts to burn.

I tread where fear and wonder meet,
Each heartbeat feels a rhythm fleet.
The echoes of the past can fade,
As future dreams begin to wade.

The whispers of the unseen guide,
In depths where mysteries abide.
With faith, I forge through shadowed ways,
Into the light of brighter days.

Uncharted lands await my feet,
Where every pause feels bittersweet.
Yet through the trials, strength will grow,
In every step, the seeds I sow.

Embracing all that life presents,
I walk with joy, despite the tense.
In steps unknown, I find my way,
Emerging bold with each new day.

Grounded in Adventure

I find my roots in shifting sand,
With dreams that shape my journey's brand.
Each moment holds a hint of grace,
As I explore this sacred space.

The call of forests, mountains high,
Invites me forth beneath the sky.
With every leap, I touch the ground,
In nature's arms, my strength is found.

The rivers flow, with stories spun,
Of paths once taken, adventures won.
I gather treasures from the trails,
In every heartbeat, freedom sails.

From quiet woods to roaring seas,
The earth reveals its mysteries.
I stand amazed as visions blend,
In adventures where I will transcend.

Grounded firm, yet spirits soar,
In every step, I long for more.
With open heart and willing hands,
I greet the magic of new lands.

Crossroads of Tomorrow

Where paths entwine beneath the stars,
Choices shimmer, light from afar.
Winds of change softly call,
Each direction leads to a new sprawl.

With every step, the heart shall guide,
Illuminating the dreams inside.
Voices echo in the silent night,
Revealing truths hidden from sight.

In shadows cast by fears we face,
We seek the warmth of hope's embrace.
Hands of time hold our souls tight,
As we choose our fate, day or night.

Every glance points to the way,
In the dawn of a brand new day.
Beneath the sky, we rise and fall,
At the crossroads, we heed the call.

With courage found deep in the soul,
We carve the journey, make us whole.
Every moment, a choice we claim,
In this dance, we find our flame.

Pathways Forged in Spirit

Through the forest, whispers weave,
In the heart, we learn to believe.
Abundant light flows through the trees,
Guiding souls upon the breeze.

With every step upon this ground,
Our essence, there, profoundly found.
In the silence, hear the call,
From the roots, we rise and fall.

Journey on with open hearts,
Embrace the pain and joyful parts.
For every pathway that we find,
Is a testament to hearts aligned.

Streams of wisdom, softly flow,
In the spirit, learn and grow.
Beneath the stars, we take our flight,
As pathways shine in the night.

Together forged in light and trust,
Creating bonds that turn to dust.
Yet in the echoes, we remain,
Pathways sung in sweet refrain.

Wandering Whispers

In the stillness, secrets bloom,
Wandering whispers fill the room.
Where shadows dance upon the wall,
Echoes linger, a silver thrall.

Through the night, we softly tread,
Guided by the words unsaid.
Each moment fleeting, yet so near,
In every breath, a tale we hear.

Footsteps trace the paths of yore,
Mapping dreams we can't ignore.
In the silence, stories blend,
Whispers of hope, a timeless friend.

As the stars paint stories bright,
We wander through the velvet night.
Carried in the arms of fate,
Each whisper calls to contemplate.

Letting go, embracing love,
Freedom shines from skies above.
In wandering, we find our peace,
Through whispered paths, our souls release.

Hopes Left Behind

In the echoes of yesterday,
Hopes linger, softly sway.
Though time moves, we still recall,
Moments cherished, one and all.

Through the trials that we've faced,
Pieces of our dreams, now chased.
Yet in every loss, we gain,
The strength to rise from the pain.

A canvas painted with our tears,
Reflections of our hopes and fears.
In shadows cast by fading light,
Memories burn against the night.

Embers glow of dreams once bright,
Guiding stars in the darkest flight.
Though hopes may fade, they never die,
For in our hearts, they learn to fly.

With every heartbeat, a new start,
Renewed visions not far apart.
In the journey of what's ahead,
We carry dreams where hopes have fled.

Aligning with New Dawn

In morning light, dreams take flight,
The world awakens, pure and bright.
Hope unfurls its tender wings,
As nature sings of fresh new springs.

With every step, a path we trace,
Together in this sacred space.
Hearts align with the rising sun,
Embracing what we have begun.

Soft whispers guide our gentle way,
Through shadows that once held us at bay.
Each dawn a chance, a promise made,
A symphony that will not fade.

The past will fade, as time will show,
New visions rise from depths below.
In every glance, a story spun,
Awakening the joy, the fun.

With open hearts, we step ahead,
Leaving behind what once was said.
The sky ignites with colors bold,
As future paths begin to unfold.

A Pilgrimage of Purpose

We journey forth with faith in hand,
A canvas stretched across the land.
With every step, we seek to find,
The calling deep within our mind.

Mountains rise and valleys spread,
With every heart, a word unsaid.
Through trials, joys, and tests we roam,
In every heart, we find a home.

The stars above, they guide our way,
Through darkest night and break of day.
With purpose strong, we light the fire,
An ember of our heart's desire.

Each moment lived, a lesson learned,
For every bridge, a pain once burned.
Together we will forge the light,
A tapestry of hope in flight.

As time unfolds, we shall be bold,
In every quest, our spirits gold.
A pilgrimage of love, profound,
With every footstep, purpose found.

The Canvas Underfoot

Beneath our feet, the earth is vast,
A canvas rich with tales amassed.
Each step we take, a brushstroke clear,
In colors bright, our dreams appear.

The whispers of the wind do play,
As memories dance in light of day.
With every path, we leave a mark,
Inspired by whispers in the dark.

The hills we climb, the rivers cross,
In every gain, we find the loss.
Yet still we paint with vibrant hue,
And create a world where hope is true.

In silence, we find voices loud,
In strides, we weave the heart's proud shroud.
A tapestry beneath our feet,
Artistry in every heartbeat.

So let us trace this ground we roam,
Each step a word, each pause a poem.
In unity, our vision clear,
Together weaving dreams held dear.

Steps into the Infinite

With each new dawn, the journey starts,
As open minds embrace new arts.
We tread on paths both wide and narrow,
In search of truth, our hearts like arrows.

The universe unfolds, so vast,
Embracing moments, unsurpassed.
In stillness, we hear the call,
To rise, connect, and never fall.

With every breath, the cosmos breathes,
In harmony, our spirit weaves.
The echoes of the old and new,
Guide us to what is pure and true.

Dancing stars above our heads,
Illuminate the paths we tread.
Through shadows, light, and dreams entwined,
We find the infinite in the mind.

Together we will forge ahead,
In unity, our souls are fed.
With every step, we boldly see,
The endless possibilities that be.

Journeying Forward

With each step, a dream in sight,
The road ahead, both dark and bright.
Carrying hopes, I traverse wide,
In the heart, my soul's guide.

Through the valleys, steep and low,
I gather strength, let courage grow.
Whispers of fate, calling me near,
In every echo, I conquer fear.

Mountains loom, yet I will climb,
Seizing moments, lost in time.
Every stumble, a tale to tell,
In the journey, I find my spell.

The map is drawn by hands unseen,
Through tangled paths, I weave the green.
With open heart, I embrace the chase,
In every turn, I find my place.

So onward still, I raise my gaze,
In twilight's glow, through life's maze.
Each dawn, a promise, sweet and bold,
In the journey, my spirit unfolds.

Footprints in the Dawn

Footprints lie where dreams began,
In morning light, I make my stand.
Each step whispers, a tale of old,
In dawn's embrace, my heart is bold.

Waves of light, a shimmering dance,
I chase the sun, my soul in trance.
Silent echoes from the past,
In every moment, shadows cast.

In the dew, a promise shines,
Nature's voice in gentle lines.
The path ahead, with hope I tread,
Onward, through whispers, I am led.

As skies unfold, my fears take flight,
With every bated breath, I write.
In the soft glow, the day awakes,
A dream renewed, as the dawn breaks.

These footprints mark the way I roam,
In every step, I find my home.
Through the dawn's embrace, I will be,
A wanderer, forever free.

The Path Unfolds

In fields of gold where the wildflowers sway,
Each step taken, I find my way.
The path unfolds, slow and wide,
In tender light, I walk with pride.

Beneath the trees, secrets reside,
In nature's arms, my fears subside.
The whispers of wind, a calming song,
In every heartbeat, I belong.

Clouds drift softly, a painter's brush,
In the silence, my thoughts hush.
With open eyes, I seek and find,
In twilight's glow, the stars aligned.

Moments linger, yet swiftly pass,
Time a river, a mirror of glass.
Through shadows and light, I'll journey on,
Believing always, hope has drawn.

Each bend of the road, a chance to grow,
With every breath, new seasons flow.
In this vast world, I choose to believe,
The path unfolds, I will achieve.

Echoes of the Wanderer

Wandering souls, we move with grace,
In every heartbeat, we find our place.
Echoes call from deep within,
In silent moments, journeys begin.

Paths untraveled lead us near,
In the distance, I hear the clear.
Songs of the past, sweet and low,
Guide my feet, where shadows flow.

Mountains rise to greet the skies,
Beneath their watch, my spirit flies.
In every valley, tales reside,
The echoes of dreams, my heart's guide.

Upon the winds, whispers dance,
In fleeting glances lies my chance.
Through every storm, I find my way,
The echoes lead, come what may.

So let me roam, and let me soar,
In echoes of yore, forevermore.
With open heart, I'll heed the sound,
In every echo, I am found.

The Art of Moving Forward

Life is a canvas, colors bright,
Brush strokes of hope in morning light.
With every challenge, we find our way,
Inspiration blooms, come what may.

Each setback a lesson, each fear a guide,
Waves of courage swell with pride.
Step by step, we rise anew,
The art of moving forward, always true.

Winds may whisper doubts to hear,
But love and strength will banish fear.
Through valleys deep, we will prevail,
As dreams unfold, we set our sail.

In the heart lies a spark untamed,
A dance of spirit, forever named.
With every heartbeat, we soar above,
Painted in courage, guided by love.

So let the journey stretch and bend,
Embrace the mountains, climb, ascend.
Each moment a chapter, a page unturned,
In the art of moving forward, we've learned.

Every Step a Story

In the quiet dawn, we start anew,
Paths unfolding, skies so blue.
With every step, a tale unfolds,
Whispers of dreams in the morning cold.

Each footfall echoes, true and clear,
Moments captured, both far and near.
Joy and sorrow intertwined,
Every step a story, life defined.

The winding roads may twist and turn,
Lessons of patience, we shall learn.
In laughter shared and burdens shared,
A map of memories, love declared.

Through fields of gold and shadows cast,
Each heartbeat echoes, ties amassed.
In every stumble, in every rise,
Every step a story, no disguise.

As twilight comes, with stars aglow,
We trace the paths of all we know.
In every journey, we find our place,
Every step a story, an embrace.

Footprints in the Sand

Along the shore, where waves do play,
Footprints linger, then wash away.
Each step a moment, memories grand,
Footprints in the sand, life's rich strand.

The tide it rises, erasing past,
Yet lessons learned are meant to last.
In sunlit days and storms that rage,
Footprints in the sand, the heart's own page.

With every grain, a tale unfolds,
Of dreams we chased, of hearts so bold.
In the dance of surf, we feel the thrill,
Footprints in the sand, the world stands still.

A journey shared, with loved ones near,
In laughter and trust, we conquer fear.
Though time may wash away the land,
We leave behind, our footprints stand.

As twilight dims and stars appear,
We hold each moment, cherished and dear.
In cycles of life, we understand,
Footprints in the sand, forever planned.

Rhythm of the Road

Beneath the sky, the asphalt gleams,
Every journey born from dreams.
With wheels that turn, we chase the light,
The rhythm of the road, pure delight.

Each mile a memory, moments flare,
In laughter's echo, in fresh night air.
With every bend, a new chance waits,
The rhythm of the road, life celebrates.

Through mountains high and valleys wide,
Adventure calls, we seek to ride.
In every sunset, colors blend,
The rhythm of the road, our faithful friend.

With open hearts and hopes so grand,
We wander freely, hand in hand.
Each journey crafted, each tale we wrote,
The rhythm of the road, in every note.

So let the wheels spin, the engine roar,
With every adventure, we crave for more.
In the dance of travel, forever bestowed,
We find our freedom in the rhythm of the road.

Traces of Tenacity

In shadows cast by doubts that loom,
The heart ignites with quiet bloom.
Through trials faced, the spirit soars,
A whispered promise, strength restores.

Each step we take amidst the strife,
We carve our path, we shape our life.
With every fall, we rise anew,
Resilient souls, forever true.

The scars we wear, a badge of pride,
In every tear, our hopes abide.
Through storms we weather, through pain we see,
The beauty found in tenacity.

As dawn breaks clear, the past we trace,
With steadfast hearts, we find our space.
In every struggle, wisdom grows,
With tenacity, the spirit glows.

The Dance of Footsteps

Upon the path where echoes sing,
The dance of footsteps starts to spring.
With every beat, the earth will sigh,
As memories twirl, the moments fly.

The rhythm found in nature's grace,
A gentle sway, a soft embrace.
With laughter high, with spirits free,
We find our way in harmony.

Across the fields where wildflowers grow,
The vibrant hues begin to show.
In every turn, a story told,
The dance of footprints, brave and bold.

From mountains high to valleys deep,
In every step, our dreams we keep.
With every leap, we dare to tread,
The dance of life, where hearts are led.

Wanderlust Whispers

In whispered winds, the travels call,
With every breeze, I hear it all.
The map of dreams, unfolding wide,
A journey waits where hearts collide.

Beneath the stars, the compass sways,
Guiding souls through mysterious ways.
The road ahead, a canvas clear,
With wanderlust, we shed our fear.

Each step we take, a story brief,
In every turn, we find belief.
With open hearts, we roam the land,
In nature's arms, we make our stand.

Through mountains tall and rivers wide,
We seek the truth, we seek the ride.
In every heartbeat, every sigh,
Wanderlust whispers, never shy.

Along the Uncharted Way

In realms unknown where dreams intwine,
We tread the path, the stars align.
With courage strong, we press ahead,
Along the uncharted way, we spread.

The horizon calls, a beckoning light,
A symphony of day and night.
With open minds and daring souls,
We journey forth, embracing unknown roles.

Through forests deep and valleys low,
Each twist and turn ignites the glow.
In every moment, chance we take,
Along the uncharted way, we wake.

With every heartbeat, new paths unfold,
In the tales of life, we dare be bold.
The map unwritten, the stories sway,
Together we roam, come what may.

The Rhythm of Progress

In the dawn of the morning light,
Steps are taken, futures bright.
Each heartbeat, a pulse of change,
Together we rise, deep and strange.

With dreams as wide as the endless sky,
We soar on wings, we learn to fly.
Facing fears that come our way,
Strength in unity, come what may.

Every challenge, a dance we share,
In the rhythm, we find our flair.
Paths entwined, like a woven thread,
For progress whispers, 'move ahead.'

Voices joined in harmonious song,
Together we belong, we are strong.
In the tapestry of hopes and schemes,
We build our future, we chase our dreams.

Let the journey guide our souls,
For in each step, this story unfolds.
With courage and love, we embark anew,
In the rhythm of life, we are true.

Following the Heart's Compass

In the depths of the silent night,
A whisper calls, soft and light.
Maps unrolled, paths spread wide,
With the heart as our trusty guide.

Flowing rivers, mountains tall,
Every step, we heed the call.
Through thorny bushes and open fields,
The heart's compass gently yields.

Moments stolen in the sun's warm glow,
Courage blooms where love does grow.
Trusting the journey, embracing fate,
With every choice, we create our state.

The stars above, our dreams ignite,
Chasing shadows into the light.
Learning from losses, celebrating wins,
In the depths of our souls, true life begins.

Paths converge, hearts intertwined,
In each echo, a truth we find.
Letting love guide the way we roam,
In the compass of hearts, we are home.

A Tapestry of Trails

Through winding woods and valleys deep,
We weave the dreams that we will keep.
Each trail we travel, a story spun,
In the fabric of life, we are one.

Golden threads of laughter and tears,
Stitching moments across the years.
With every step, a new design,
In the tapestry, our spirits shine.

Mountains high and rivers wide,
In this journey, we will abide.
Through storms that test and winds that sway,
We hold our ground; we find our way.

In the quilt of friendship, love, and grace,
Every thread finds its rightful place.
A patchwork of memories, vibrant and bright,
Illuminating our shared plight.

Let the trails speak in whispers sweet,
For every finish brings a new feat.
Through the chapters, old and new,
In this tapestry, we craft what's true.

Dancing Along the Journey

With each step, a dance we sway,
In rhythm, we find our way.
Whispers of joy in the breeze,
As the world around us frees.

Embracing moments, fleeting and rare,
With laughter, we lighten the air.
In the cadence of heartbeats, we play,
Dancing along, come what may.

Underneath the twilight's hue,
Stars in motion, dreams anew.
With hands held tight, we twirl and glide,
In every leap, our hopes reside.

Through valleys dim and mountains bright,
Every turn becomes a flight.
In the sway of the moon's soft glow,
We find the path, as we dance flow.

With courage, we face the unknown,
In this journey, we've grown.
Together we weave this beautiful art,
Dancing along, heart to heart.

Journey's Gentle Rhythm

Soft whispers guide my way,
In the dawn of a new day.
Footsteps on a path unknown,
Each moment feels like home.

Breezes carry tales of old,
Stories in the sun's warm gold.
With each breath, I find my truth,
In the dance of fleeting youth.

Mountains rise, and rivers flow,
Through the heart, where dreams do grow.
Nature's pulse, a steady beat,
Mapping out my journey sweet.

Stars above begin to twinkle,
In their light, my hopes do sprinkle.
The night's embrace, so vast and deep,
In its quiet, secrets keep.

Path ahead may twist and weave,
Yet I trust what I believe.
With each step, my spirit sings,
In the joy that journey brings.

Echoes Behind Me

Footsteps fade into the past,
Lessons learned, shadows cast.
Whispers linger in the air,
Reminding me to pause and care.

Faces in memories reside,
Guiding me through the wild tide.
Each echo holds a piece of me,
Carved in time, a legacy.

Through valleys low and mountains high,
I hear the softest lullaby.
Every choice, a note in song,
Together, they make me strong.

Fading glimpses of long-lost dreams,
Flow like rivers, or so it seems.
Yet, I rise with each new dawn,
With courage, I will carry on.

What was once is now well known,
In my heart, I've brightly grown.
Echoes whisper, "Let it be,"
As I dance toward what I see.

The Path Unfolds

A winding road beneath my feet,
With every choice, I feel complete.
Sunshine bathes the way ahead,
In hope and light, my spirit's fed.

Branches sway, as if to greet,
The wanderer, who dares to meet.
With open heart, I trace my steps,
Finding joy in each new depth.

Clouds may gather, storms descend,
Yet every struggle seems to mend.
In the chaos, beauty blooms,
Life reveals its many rooms.

With gentle hands, the world unfolds,
A tale of wonder, yet untold.
In each turn, adventures gleam,
Awakening the deepest dream.

So, I walk, embracing fate,
Each moment shaped, a woven state.
On this path, I feel the call,
In the journey, I grow tall.

Cadence of Courage

In the depths of night, I rise,
Fearless heart beneath the skies.
With every breath, I stand my ground,
In the silence, strength is found.

Though shadows loom and doubts arise,
I keep my gaze on distant highs.
The rhythm of my beating heart,
A melody that sets apart.

Stepping forth, I break the chains,
In the struggle, life remains.
Each challenge faced, a note in time,
Together woven, strong and prime.

Together with the stars, I soar,
In the night, I find my core.
The cadence of my inner fight,
Guides me home through darkest night.

So I march, with fierce resolve,
With love and strength, I will evolve.
In the dance of life, I see,
The courage blossoming in me.

The Road Less Traveled

In quiet woods where whispers roam,
I found a path that led me home.
With every step, my heart would race,
Embracing dreams, I found my place.

The sun would rise, a golden beam,
Illuminating every dream.
The road was tough, yet sweetly wild,
Awakening the inner child.

With every turn, new sights appeared,
Strengthened by both hope and fear.
I journeyed on, my spirit free,
A testament to who I'd be.

Though shadows lurked along the way,
I held my ground, come what may.
Each step I took, a story told,
In whispered winds of brave and bold.

So here I stand, with head held high,
The road less traveled caught my eye.
In every choice, a lesson learned,
For every path, my heart has yearned.

Navigating Horizons

Beneath the endless sky so blue,
I chart my course, my heart so true.
Each wave that crashes, every tide,
A guide for dreams tucked deep inside.

With stars as maps, I sail the night,
Chasing visions in the light.
Horizons stretch, both vast and wide,
In depths of night, my dreams abide.

The compass whispers, winds will call,
Through storms and calm, I stand up tall.
A sailor brave, I find my way,
In fading dusk and blooming day.

As shores approach, new worlds unfold,
With every journey, stories told.
In every wave, a promise shines,
The heart's true map, where love aligns.

So onward still, with courage fierce,
Navigating dreams that gently pierce.
With every step, horizons blend,
In every journey, find the end.

Embracing the Earth Beneath

In fields of green, I run and play,
Where sunbeams dance and children sway.
The earth beneath, so rich and strong,
In every heartbeat, nature's song.

With every flower, with every tree,
Life around whispers, "Come and see!"
The soil cradles dreams untold,
In gentle hands, the earth I hold.

Mountains rise where shadows fall,
Nature's beauty, standing tall.
With every breath, I feel the ground,
In vibrant life, my soul is found.

From rivers flowing, to skies so vast,
Every moment, a spell is cast.
Embrace the earth, her spirit pure,
In every heart, her love endures.

So here I stand, with arms spread wide,
Embracing earth, my faithful guide.
In every step, the world I greet,
With grateful heart, I feel complete.

Shadows of the Past

In quiet corners, shadows creep,
Whispered secrets that I keep.
Each memory, both sharp and sweet,
Weaves a tapestry beneath my feet.

Echoes linger of laughter and tears,
Reflections caught within the years.
The past, a friend, or foe described,
In stories held, historically inscribed.

As twilight falls, the shadows grow,
Beneath the surface, feelings flow.
With every step, a haunted trace,
I walk the line of time and space.

Yet from the dark, new light will shine,
In lessons learned, my soul's design.
Though shadows cast their fleeting shade,
In every trial, my strength cascades.

So I embrace both light and dark,
For in the silence, ignites a spark.
The shadows fade but never part,
Forever etched within my heart.

Striding Towards Hope

With every step, the dawn will break,
A whisper soft, the night will wake.
Carried dreams on gentle wings,
In future light, my spirit sings.

Though shadows stretch across my way,
Each path I walk leads to the day.
A heart that's open, brave, and true,
Guides me onward, ever new.

Through valleys low and hills so steep,
In twilight moments, courage seeps.
With steadfast breath, I rise and stand,
The dawn awaits, a promised land.

I gather strength from those who've fought,
Their stories woven, battles sought.
In unity, we share this road,
Together lightens every load.

So here I stride with hope in hand,
Ready to face what truth has planned.
Each footfall echoes, loud and clear,
The future shines, it draws me near.

A Walk Beneath the Stars

Beneath the vast, enchanting sky,
I wander where the soft winds sigh.
Each twinkle tells a tale untold,
In silver light, my heart feels bold.

The gentle brush of night's cool air,
Holds secrets that the stars all share.
I follow paths where dreams reside,
On this celestial, glowing ride.

With every step, the quiet hum,
Of distant worlds, I hear them come.
In whispers soft, they guide my way,
Through shadowed night into the day.

I pause beneath a comet's flight,
Inspiring awe, a fleeting sight.
The universe, so vast and wide,
Reminds me hope I cannot hide.

Together with the moonlit glow,
I roam through realms, both high and low.
With every glance, my spirit soars,
A journey boundless, forevermore.

Paths of Perseverance

In fields where weary travelers tread,
Each step, a challenge, softly led.
Through thorns and stones, my feet will march,
With every heartbeat, fears I arch.

I pause to rest, yet never yield,
With grit and grace, my wounds are healed.
The road is long, but heart is strong,
In moments dark, I find the song.

The sun will rise, the storm will pass,
This strength within, a sacred glass.
Through trials faced, I will not bend,
Each path I walk, a steadfast friend.

With every bend, new hope appears,
For every laugh, I've shed my tears.
The journey waits; I will not fear,
For every day, a new frontier.

In unison, my spirit fights,
Across the shadows, towards the lights.
With persistence leading every turn,
The flame within, it will not burn.

Finding Balance in Motion

In life's sweet dance, I seek my place,
With every movement, find my grace.
The rhythm flows in beats so bright,
Through twists and turns, I find the light.

Each sway and step, a lesson learned,
In gentle currents, I've discerned.
With heart aligned and mind in tune,
I chase the dreams beneath the moon.

I balance fears with hopes in hand,
On shaky ground, I choose to stand.
In uncertainty, I find my way,
With mutual trust, I seize the day.

The world spins on, yet I adhere,
To inner calm, I hold it dear.
With every breath, I weave and flow,
In harmony, my spirit grows.

So here I move with steady grace,
Through every challenge, I embrace.
In rhythm, find my center, true,
In motion's dance, I start anew.

Finding Solace in Motion

In the stillness of the night,
I seek the rhythm of my heart.
With every step, a whisper sings,
A dance where shadows play their part.

The world around begins to fade,
As I embrace the soothing breeze.
Footfalls echo on the path,
In motion, I find subtle peace.

Wandering where the quiet beckons,
With nature's breath, my spirit sways.
Among the trees, I lose my cares,
And find the light within the haze.

Stars above, a guiding force,
In darkness, they ignite my soul.
With every stride, new strength I gain,
In movement, I become quite whole.

Each turn a story unfolds,
Each moment sealed in time's embrace.
Through winding paths, I roam and tread,
Motion becomes my sacred space.

Steps Underneath the Stars

Beneath a tapestry of night,
I walk where wishes softly gleam.
Each step imbued with dreams and light,
In the silence, I dare to dream.

Moonlit rays guide my way,
Whispering tales of long ago.
With every footfall, I convey,
A history of ebb and flow.

The cosmos watches from above,
As I traverse this sacred ground.
In nature's arms, I feel the love,
With every heartbeat, I am found.

The stars align with paths I take,
Chasing echoes of forgotten lore.
In starlit dance, I dare to wake,
As I wander, I'm always more.

Steps beneath the cosmic show,
A journey wrapped in twilight's song.
Through shadows deep and rivers slow,
In the night, I feel I belong.

Echoing Through Eternity

In the silence that surrounds,
I hear echoes from the past.
Each whisper carries, time unwound,
An endless song that's built to last.

Moments lost, yet here they stay,
In the chambers of my mind.
As twilight dawns, they lead the way,
Through shadows where my heart can find.

Pathways tread by souls before,
Footsteps linger in the air.
Their stories weave forevermore,
A tapestry of love and care.

Time reflects in every glance,
An essence rich, a vibrant hue.
With every step, I join the dance,
In echoes deep, I start anew.

The dialogue of years gone by,
In whispers soft, they call my name.
Through history, I learn to fly,
Through every heart, I feel the flame.

The Map of My Soles

Across the earth, my journey flows,
Mapped by the trails beneath my feet.
With every step, a story grows,
In rhythms where my heart will meet.

Through fields where wildflowers bloom,
And city streets that hum with life.
My soles imprint their soft perfume,
In every heartbeat, joy or strife.

A compass drawn in sands of time,
A narrative in every stride.
The world unfolds in scented rhyme,
As I embrace the path I ride.

Each footprint echoes where I've been,
In rivers deep and mountains high.
The map of my soles, a quiet kin,
In every journey, I learn to fly.

In each direction lies a dream,
In every corner, hope anew.
With open heart, I join the stream,
The map of my soles guides me true.